Live for a Living

Goals for Developing Your Career Path to Work Smarter, Not Harder

Koso Brown

Contents

Introduction

It is crucial to take action based on a clear definition of life when looking for extraterrestrial life. According to the definition of life in the 20th century, cells that are capable of self-replication, metabolism, and mutation are those that allow genetic information to alter and allow for evolution. Current definitions of life are based on twentieth-century statistical mechanics, physics, and chemistry, which ignore the crucial role that communication plays in life and instead view it as functioning like a machine. According to recent observations, meaningful communication that is context-dependent and network development (and regulation) are essential to all living species.

Instead of originating from mistakes, evolutionary important novel nucleotide sequences now seem to have come from social agents like viruses, their parasitic relatives, and associated RNA networks. A new definition of life for the twenty-first century can be arrived at by applying the known characteristics of natural languages and communication, wherein communicative interactions are fundamental to all aspects of life processes. For a new definition of life to outperform the story of the twentieth century, it must incorporate the most recent scientific findings regarding the interactions between viruses, RNA networks, and cells.

Chapter 1: Life and Career

You may hear from friends and relatives that your search for meaningful employment is futile. They'll argue that other matters are more significant. They'll claim that earning money and working are meaningless endeavors.

This is akin to asserting that appearances are unimportant, so going to the gym is pointless. It's just not the purpose. Exercise has several advantages beyond just improving one's physical appearance. These include increased energy, happier moods, better sleep, reduced stress, and more.

A career is as essential to life as anything else. Furthermore, we cannot neglect a significant aspect of our lives, such as our income, relationships, careers, or health.

We'll talk about the effect a person's career has on their wellbeing in this piece. It is necessary to have this knowledge since obstacles will unavoidably arise on our path to meaningful employment. Understanding the significance of a career in life can aid in overcoming obstacles.

1. Your social life will be defined by your work.

I realized that teaching wasn't for me when I was a substitute teacher and saw the other educators. It was the people I would be working with, not the job, that was on my mind. Let me start by saying that teachers are good people—many of my closest friends work in education! Simply put, most of them seemed pleased to work, go home, and then start over the next day at the schools where I was employed. The fact that none of them seemed to like it and instead only had complaints about the kids alarmed me even more. I only had this personal experience.

2. It gives guidance and meaning.

Not only did I feel unhappy while working at jobs I

detested, but I also found it impossible to envision a time when I would work at jobs I liked. I thought I had nowhere to go and that I would spend the rest of my life doing work I detested. Humans require accountability. When someone is depending on us, we give it our all. We have to believe that the world is changing as a result of our actions.

Our lives are given direction and meaning by our work. We are aware that there is a community of people depending on us when we do meaningful work. a location that needs us. a location where our actions count.

3. It's an essential component of who you are.

Everyone I meet at a gathering always asks, "What do you do? "Take note of the way they pose the question. They don't inquire, "What do you do for a living?" or "What are you employed for?" In essence, they are asking, "What do you do in life? "This question used to aggravate me. I detested what I was doing, which is why. It makes sense that the majority of us wince when asked what we do since we are unable to respond with pride.

Our careers have a big role in who we are. We typically own multiple identities. I identify with my work, but I also identify as a learner, a fitness enthusiast, a friend, a brother, a son, etc. One of the main components of our identities is our work. When we first meet someone, it's the first question we ask and receive. This is because it makes up a sizable chunk of our lives. It pretty much sums up everything else. It's the one you spend the most time being among all of your identities. You therefore don't want to ignore it.

4. It influences your identity at home.

Don't believe that your employment won't impact your identity outside of the workplace lot of people who detest their employment often start bad behaviors.

A few of those behaviors include emotional eating, drinking,

using drugs, watching TV, experiencing despair, or just becoming angry easily. When our job isn't fulfilling, we have to find other ways to get by. These coping techniques may have detrimental consequences. They entail dodging the problem as opposed to confronting it head-on.

Your life outside of work will be better and you will be more optimistic and energetic if your career is in line with who you are. Your loved ones will be able to tell the difference between your happy and unhappy moments.

5. Much of your life is your career.

Your work makes up almost half of your life when sleep is taken into account. That is a significant sum. That means that if you despise or are indifferent to your job, you will be indifferent to or detest it for almost half of your life. Not favorable.

Since we'll be spending a lot of time at work, it's critical to ensure that the time isn't killing you.

One should be persuaded of the significance of a career just by the fact that it occupies a sizable portion of one's life.

Chapter 2: Navigating Your Career Journey

Consider a recent travel experience. What preparations did you make for this trip? What were some of the travel, lodging, and other logistics? What were your travel goals for this trip? What did you bring with you? How much time did you spend planning this? Depending on the type of trip, organizing a trip is typically a time-consuming process, but it should also be enjoyable and fulfilling, especially if you end up having a fantastic time!

Organizing your career is similar to organizing a trip. It involves a great deal of investigation and study because there are several aspects and choices to be made. The procedure isn't one-step-only. Choosing a major doesn't automatically dictate how the rest of your life turns out, despite what many people think. At the Center for Career Development (CCD), the expression "I'm a [insert name of major] major - what can I do with that?" is frequently heard.

It appears that a major is usually correlated with a particular job route in our society. It is true that some job paths—like those in engineering and accounting—benefit from having a particular kind of school background, if not require it.

We discuss the "career development process" a lot at the CCD. What does that mean specifically? This is choosing a career or careers and making your way through them. You will engage in it for the rest of your life, and you have already begun. The process is dynamic, shifting back and forth between phases.

Even if we show it with arrows leading from one step to the next, it's crucial to remember that it's not always linear and that these steps don't happen in a tidy sequence. You will go through several stages as you learn and develop; it's a lifelong developmental process. Learning about yourself, exploring occupations, reflecting, and taking action are the essential parts that will remain the same when you leave ND. Some specifics, like selecting a major, will change. It's crucial that you understand the process today so that you may use it repeatedly as needed to manage your career efficiently. To understand more about these phases, let's take a brief look at a popular career theory.

Step 1: The first step in developing a career is to educate yourself.

One of the theories of professional decision-making that is most widely recognized was created by Dr. Donald Super (Luzzo & Severy, 2009). He was one of the first to propose that choosing a vocation is a lifelong process of personal development. He argued that a person's ability to recognize and execute their career self-concept—which is made up of their values, interests, personality, and skills— determines their level of career satisfaction and success.

The premise is that an individual's best employment choices are ones that enable them to live out as much of their self-concept as they can. A person is likely to run into a brick wall in their work if they choose to concentrate solely on one or two aspects of their self-concept. For instance, if someone just concentrates on skill, they can discover that their personality is off or that their passion isn't aligned with their values. For a while, that person can continue in the career, but ultimately, they might begin to feel unsatisfied and possibly burn out. This emphasizes how important it is to take into account values, interests, personality, and talents while choosing a career.

This gets us to the first phase in the above visual: self-discovery. Making wise career decisions requires first knowing yourself, your values, interests, personality, and skills (VIPS). The only way to discover more about yourself is to take a chance and get out and live! Your VIPS have already begun to take shape as a result of everything you've done thus far and the relationships you've had. Classes, extracurriculars, employment, volunteering, research, and other experiences all count toward this; even things that don't seem to have anything to do with a career can reveal a lot about your interests, values, and preferred methods of interacting with the outside world.

Step 2: Learn About What You Enjoy and Participate

Step 2: Research What We understand that first-year students often find it difficult to find opportunities to get engaged on campus because they are primarily focused on keeping themselves afloat, making new friends, and performing well in their academics. However, it's crucial to look for other opportunities to get involved that work for you as much as possible. Joining clubs exclusive to a certain job is not required. You Appreciate and Participate.

Additionally, you can participate in your resident hall and its many offerings by joining the hall council. However, exercise caution when going too far—participating in campus life is primarily about quality, not quantity. Recall that sleep is equally vital!

Step 3: Look into Careers

You can start looking outside at career prospects once you have explored enjoyable majors, become active, and conducted introspection around your VIPS. Since there are so many different professions and professional options, it's best to avoid setting too many early boundaries for yourself. It will help you focus a little bit because you probably already know which fields don't interest you, but it's still a good idea to look well beyond that. This is the point at which step 1's self-evaluation is useful. Once you start exploring, you'll be better able to determine what profession sectors would be a suitable fit for you because you will have a better understanding of your VIPS. To get started on your research, the CCD offers a wealth of information and tools.

The Value of Professional Planning

You've heard the phrase "plan your career" a thousand times. However, why is it so crucial? Career planning involves more than just finding your ideal work; it also entails defining your passions and abilities, creating professional and personal objectives, and learning how to overcome unavoidable failures.

It is also closely related to retirement planning and financial planning. By taking charge of your professional path, you're creating the way for personal development and fulfillment in addition to safeguarding your future.

Understanding the Importance of Career Planning

Comprehending the significance of career planning is vital for your job advancement. By exploring many career options, you can find ones that fit your beliefs, interests, and skill set. A well-organized strategy that outlines objectives and the activities necessary to reach them improves job satisfaction.

Consider career planning as an effective development roadmap. Your desire drives the trip, and the plan gives you direction. Your journey will go more smoothly if your strategy is more comprehensive. Thus, don't undervalue the importance of career preparation, and start shaping your future right now!

Recall that living a happy working life involves more than just making money—it involves enjoying what you do daily.

Creating both short- and long-term objectives

Setting up short- and long-term goals involves more than merely checking boxes. It serves as a dynamic road map for your goals, guiding you through an exciting universe of opportunities.

Imagine yourself embarking on a journey where each step is accompanied by milestones that help you get closer to your final destination. That is how goal visualization works.

Establishing specific goals will enable you to create achievement tactics that are most effective for you. These tactics are what keep your career moving forward and help you succeed.

When planning your career, knowing your hobbies and talents is crucial. It assists you in selecting occupations based on your interests that complement your innate abilities and passions.

Consider these steps:

1. **Research:** Explore career alternatives that align with your interests and skill set.

2. **Self-reflection:** Think about what gives you energy, the things you do well, or the areas that people perceive as your strong points.

3. **Skill assessment techniques:** To determine your skills accurately, use online resources, tests, or the services of a professional coach.

Identifying Your Interests

Exploring what genuinely interests you deeply is similar to finding a source of inspiration that points you in the direction of employment you'll enjoy and be successful at. Finding your passions and what excites, inspires, and motivates you is the goal of passion research, not only turning pastimes into careers. It can be a nontraditional vocation that goes against the grain of society yet fits in with your goals and essential principles.

Following these passions will help you find rewarding careers that represent your unique self. Don't let fear of instability or uncertainty prevent you from taking chances or from choosing unconventional routes. Rather, bravely go after what ignites your soul.

Keep in mind that having a fulfilling daily routine is just as crucial for good career planning as having the possibility to earn a lot of money.

Chapter 3: The Role of Education in Career Planning

It's a statement you've undoubtedly heard a thousand times: knowledge is the key to success. But have you ever given it any thought as to how it would affect your future? It's your first step toward achieving ambitions you never even knew you had; it's not only about getting degrees and learning new skills.

Education is a vital component of career preparation and has several advantages. It assists with completing educational gaps that would otherwise impede your advancement in the workplace. Coordinating your academic achievements with your preferred professional route guarantees degree relevance. Finally, education opens doors to knowledge extension and personal development that go beyond work proficiency.

The Significance of Work Experience and Internships

Work experience and internships are essential in forming your career. They give you useful information and abilities. They also assist you in better preparing for your future career by assisting you in comprehending the realities of the labor market.

These encounters can advance your career development. They are regarded as essential components of any fruitful professional plan.

Why Internships Are Beneficial

It's a fact that internships are more than simply a way to enhance your resume; they're the key to launching your ideal career! They provide exposure to a variety of industries that you cannot obtain elsewhere. You'll get the opportunity to learn about many professions and sectors, which will enable you to hone your professional path.

Additionally, internships offer income in a variety of forms. Yes, there may be a generous stipend, but consider other factors as well. No salary can compare to the experience gained. Additionally, you build important networks and professional skills that frequently result in employment opportunities.

In summary, internships play a critical role in determining your future professional pathways and choices. Therefore, don't undervalue their significance when organizing your professional path—it might well save your life!

How to choose a career

Throughout your working life, you'll continually devise a strategy to manage your learning and advancement: a career plan. Its four stages are designed to assist you in visualizing the steps you need to take and the methods by which you need to implement these steps to reach your career goals.

A career plan has four phases:

1. Determine your interests and abilities
2. investigate potential careers
3. Decide on something
4. Set attainable objectives

Chapter 4: Determine your interests and abilities

Making a career decision is important. You'll spend a large portion of your life at work, so you should make good choices if you want to like what you do, stay motivated, and reach your full potential.

You must first understand who you are. This entails evaluating your interests and values as well as your skill set.

To determine whether your knowledge and skill set are a suitable fit for the position you'd like to have, it's critical to recognize your range of abilities. Knowing what abilities, you possess also makes it easier to identify any gaps that might need to be filled to reach your professional objectives.

Enumerate all of your specialized and transferable talents, along with instances of when you've used them. When reducing the number of possibilities available to you in the next phase, an honest evaluation of your abilities, values, and interests will be helpful. Additionally, you can assess your performance concerning the qualities that employers value.

Think about your current situation, your desired destination, and your plan of action. If you're having trouble deciding on a career, start by asking yourself the following questions:

- **What skills do I have?**
- **What drives, values, and interests do I have?**
- **What was my favorite university experience?**
- **Which lifestyle am I looking for?**
- **What career goals do I have?**
- **What matters to me?**

Investigate potential careers

This is all about focusing your possibilities by doing a study on the employment market and career paths that pique your interest.

Investigate the local, national, and international employment markets to learn about the major trends in the industry you have in mind for your dream career. This will assist you in learning about additional job options and identifying roles that are growing or shrinking.

There are three main categories of employment. These are the following:

1. **Private:** partnerships, limited businesses, and lone proprietors

2. **Public:** the federal, state, and local governments, as well as their affiliated organizations

3. **Non-profit:** Often called the charity and volunteer sector, or the third sector.

You could learn about some less obvious career routes where your qualifications and talents could be relevant by looking through job profiles.

Create a shortlist of five to ten occupations, then weigh the benefits and drawbacks of each in terms of:

- Professional advancement
- Job situation
- Prerequisites for entrance
- Job description
- Similar jobs
- Pay and circumstances
- Instruction

It's also important to think about what kind of employer best suits your work ethic and personality. Are you better suited for working for yourself, for large firms, or small and medium-sized businesses (SMEs)? Now is a great time to think about internships, volunteer work, work shadowing, and work experience. Before deciding on a given professional route, they'll assist you in gaining knowledge about the sectors you're interested in.

Decide on something

You can now begin making decisions. Integrate your knowledge of yourself with what you've learned about the graduate employment market and your possibilities.

Choose the role that most appeals to you from your list of work ideas, and then make a backup plan of one or two options in case your first pick isn't available.

Consider the following questions as you help yourself to decide:

- **Do I look forward to going to work every day?**
- **Does it satisfy the majority of my needs?**

- Am I proficient in these areas?
- Do my values align with the company's?
- Are there any restrictions on my abilities, location, or finances that I should be aware of?
- Is the compensation for the position reasonable?

There are a variety of exercises you can try to help with the decision-making process if you're having trouble deciding. Writing down the benefits and drawbacks of a specific job or vocation is frequently helpful, as is performing a personal SWOT analysis:

❖ **Strengths:** What qualities, abilities, affiliations, and credentials might you provide to the position that no one else could? What distinguishes you?

❖ **Weaknesses:** What areas need improvement on your part? Are there any abilities you lack that are preventing you from succeeding in the position you want to pursue?

❖ **Prospects:** Is business expanding in your sector? Could you profit from errors made by your rivals or holes in the market?

❖ **Threats:** Could your shortcomings impede your advancement in the workplace? Is there anything else, like technological advancements, that could impede your progress?

Set attainable objectives

Your career plan should include a breakdown of your short-, medium--, and long-term goals as well as how you'll get there and what steps you need to take when. Review your progress often, particularly following the accomplishment of each short-term objective.

In case your circumstances alter, you should also create a backup plan for your professional development. Draw several different routes to your long-term objective, taking into account how you'll get past potential obstacles at each stage, such as training requirements.

Creating a stronger resume and cover letter might be your initial short-term objective. Additional short- or medium-term goals can be volunteering, attending career fairs, or taking on relevant internships.

If you feel like you need some professional reassurance, schedule a meeting with the careers office at your university to have an adviser review your career action plan and talk about your future job objectives and choices. Find out where at the university you may get support.

Lastly, keep in mind that career planning is an ongoing endeavor. Throughout your career, read over and review your goals and objectives. Don't let the goals you've set hold you back; a career plan's framework should allow you to see the obvious path to trying new things.

Chapter 5: The Importance of Career Planning

1. **Continued Learning and Growth:** A career path inspires people to value ongoing learning and development. It encourages people to look for training courses, professional certifications, and educational initiatives that advance their knowledge and skills. People enhance their marketability in the labor market and set themselves up for future development and promotion by remaining current with industry innovations and relevant.

2. **Adaptability and Flexibility:** Even if a career path gives one a sense of direction, it's crucial to recognize that pathways aren't always straight. The working world is changing, and there can be unforeseen opportunities or difficulties. Those who have a well-thought-out professional strategy, however, are better able to

alter and change course as needed. They can take advantage of new chances and pursue new directions by utilizing their transferable competencies and core skills.

3. **Making Choices and Reducing Risk:** Having a clear career path aids people in making wise decisions as they advance in their careers. It enables them to weigh the risks and compare prospective prospects to their long-term objectives. By enabling people to make decisions that are consistent with their beliefs, interests, and goals, career planning reduces the possibility of career regrets and increases the likelihood of success.

4. **Membership Retention:** Being a member of a professional association places a person at the forefront of their industry and shows a dedication to lifelong learning and growth. These factors pave the way for long-term career success. If your association can provide

members with effective tools for career planning, they will be more likely to recognize the tremendous value the association offers and will come back year after year. As a result, members of the professional associations renew their membership and enjoy happier, more prosperous professions.

5. **Clarity and Direction:** Individuals can achieve clarity and direction in their work lives through career planning. They are better able to match their professional decisions with their personal goals by using them to better understand their beliefs, interests, and skill sets. People who map out their professional paths do so with greater intention and focus, which empowers them to choose their training, education, and employment options.

6. **Growth and Development of Skills:** Individuals are encouraged to discover the skills and competencies needed to succeed in their

intended professional path through career planning. It draws attention to areas in which skill development is required and encourages people to look for growth possibilities. Through proactive skill acquisition and knowledge expansion, people improve their long-term professional prospects as well as their marketability and flexibility.

7. **Motivation and Goal-Setting:** Establishing a career path encourages motivation and makes goal-setting easier. It enables people to define goals, both short- and long-term, according to the career trajectory they want. These objectives provide benchmarks and turning points, fostering a sense of accomplishment and advancement. People are more driven to pursue professional development opportunities, take on difficult initiatives, and aim for greatness in their chosen fields when they have specific goals in mind.

Chapter 6: How to design a happy-making career path

Sadly, most people lack the knowledge necessary to make decisions at work that ultimately result in fulfillment. It is rare to find parents, educators, or mentors who encourage us to consider this or provide us with useful mental models. "When we are in our twenties, we usually only get a taste of what meaningful work is like." As such, we frequently choose careers based on false information. "We search for things that make us feel good about ourselves or that would look good on a resume," the statement goes. Nevertheless, those are not always the things that lead to happiness. You can find guidelines in this book to help you find a career—and a particular job—that you love as well as enjoy.

1. Understand your definition of "meaningful."

Do my coworkers respect me? Do I have a challenge ahead of me? Am I developing? "Do I think the mission is real?" These are the elements that will separate you from being content with your work and genuinely pleased with it. However, what each person means by "meaningful" varies. Don't limit your search to the obvious, such as title, pay, or corporate prestige. Determine the following four categories:

2. Alignment

The ideals and culture of your workplace are included in this final area. This relates to whether you feel like you belong, not whether it is the same as a mission. What values and goals do the business and the individuals you work with hold dear? How do people behave toward one another? Do they give each other hugs? eat lunch together? It's critical to enjoy the company of both your management and your coworkers. Each person's experience with these categories will be unique. This list can be used to assess particular options such as a new assignment within your existing role, a job at a different firm, or a new career path. It can assist you in making decisions.

3. Autonomy

This has to do with the pay, perks, and freedom you require to lead the kind of life you choose. This could entail having a large salary that enables you to travel to far-off places. For some, it can mean having the flexibility to work whenever and wherever you choose. Here, you should identify the lifestyle you desire and consider whether your work is assisting you in achieving it.

4. Mastery

You wish to strengthen these areas of strength. If you have a strong interpersonal skillset, for instance, you might pursue a career in psychology or marketing. In a similar vein, if you're a talented writer, you may write fiction or copy for ads. The important thing is to make use of your strengths in a way that satisfies you. "It must be something you love to do; being good at something you don't enjoy doesn't count."

5. Legacy

This relates to the tangible results of your labor. What goals do you have in mind? Most occupations indeed require you to spend some time answering emails and attending meetings, but what proof of your work do you want? Developing 80 kids' math proficiency in a year or creating six desalination plants in your career could be satisfying accomplishments. Often, this comes down to personal preference for proximity to the front lines. While some want to assist in passing the Affordable Care Act, others want to directly treat the sick.

Conclusion

Planning a career and having clear career pathways are crucial for people to follow as they navigate their professional lives. They offer direction, inspiration, goal-setting, and well-informed decision-making. A career path gives people the ability to grow, adapt, and take advantage of opportunities in addition to helping them match their goals with their chosen field. Putting time and energy into career planning is a wise move for long-term success and fulfillment in the quickly evolving workplace of today.